Ronald Reagan
The Great Communicator

Heather E. Schwartz

T0019884

Consultants

Jennifer M. Lopez, NBCT, M.S.Ed.
Teacher Specialist—History/Social Studies
Office of Curriculum & Instruction
Norfolk Public Schools

Publishing Credits

Rachelle Cracchiolo, M.S.Ed., *Publisher*
Conni Medina, M.A.Ed., *Managing Editor*
Emily R. Smith, M.A.Ed., *Content Director*
Véronique Bos, *Creative Director*
Robin Erickson, *Art Director*
Michelle Jovin, M.A., *Associate Editor*
Fabiola Sepulveda, *Graphic Designer*

TCM Teacher Created Materials

5301 Oceanus Drive
Huntington Beach, CA 92649-1030
www.tcmpub.com
ISBN 978-1-4258-5076-0
© 2020 Teacher Created Materials, Inc.

Table of Contents

Leading Man

Ronald Reagan was the 40th president of the United States. However, Reagan was famous before he became president. He was an actor first and often played heroes in movies. When he began his career in politics, people were drawn to him. Reagan was charming and upbeat. He had a good sense of humor. After two terms as governor of California, he decided to run for president. When he was elected president in 1980, many people were excited. They loved him as an actor. They were excited to see how he would run the country.

As president, Reagan was known as the "Great Communicator." That nickname came from Reagan's **wit** and charm when speaking in public. His beliefs on **communism**, the economy, and the best route for the country's future were strong and clear. And he was not afraid to take action.

Reagan left a legacy of positive change for the country and the world. Decades later, people still look back on the impact Reagan had.

Win One for the Gipper

Reagan played George Gipp in the 1940 film *Knute Rockne All American*. Gipp was a football player who played under the university's famous coach, Knute Rockne. Reagan's nickname became the "Gipper" from this role.

Screen Star

Reagan was more of a supporting actor than a leading man in Hollywood. In one famous film, *Bedtime for Bonzo*, he worked with a chimpanzee. He only played a villain once during his acting career, in the 1964 film *The Killers*.

Before the Presidency

Student Leader

Reagan showed that he was a leader early in his life. He was student body president in high school. Reagan was also the president of the student council and captain of the swim team in college.

Excellent Work Ethic

During college, Reagan worked as a dishwasher, a lifeguard, and a swim coach. These jobs helped him pay for college and support his family.

Ronald Wilson Reagan was born in Tampico, Illinois, on February 6, 1911. The Reagans were not wealthy or well connected. His father, John, was a salesman who had only a grade-school education. His mother, Nelle, taught **Sunday school** and wrote plays. As a child, Reagan spent time playing with his older brother, Neil.

As Reagan grew up, he explored many interests. He played football and basketball, joined the school drama club, and wrote for the yearbook. During summers, he worked as a lifeguard and was a true hero. He saved 77 swimmers over the course of six summers!

▲ John, Neil, Ronald, and Nelle in 1916

Reagan earned a partial football **scholarship** to attend Eureka College in Illinois. There, he joined the track team and the swim team. Reagan also joined the drama club, the school newspaper, and the yearbook. He did all this while earning a **degree** in economics and **sociology**. These years taught Reagan important lessons. He learned how to manage his time. He also learned how to focus his attention on many different things at once. These skills would help Reagan later in life.

▲ **Reagan (far right) and other members of the Eureka College swim team**

Hello, Hollywood

After Reagan graduated from college, he got a job talking about sports on the radio. He had the right kind of voice for the job and was a hit. His success in radio led to a new goal—Reagan wanted to be an actor.

In 1937, Reagan went to California to try to land a movie role. This trip turned out to be perfect timing. Warner Bros.® was looking for a new actor for an upcoming film. Reagan had the voice, looks, and charm to do the job. The studio hired him, and he started making movies.

Reagan quickly became a popular actor. Soon, his leadership skills shined once more. Reagan was elected as one of the leaders of the Screen Actors Guild (SAG). SAG protects actors' rights. In 1946, Reagan represented SAG in a very heated **dispute**. A suspected communist led the other side of the argument. This experience had a huge impact on Reagan. After this, he began to distrust communists.

◀ *Love is on the Air* was released in 1937 was Reagan's first movie role.

Due to Reagan's success in the dispute, he was elected president of SAG. Reagan soon joined a government effort to keep communism out of the film industry. People with communist ties were **blacklisted**. They lost their jobs. Reagan did not want communism in Hollywood. However, he also used his status as SAG president to help those who were wrongly accused.

Professional Patriot

Reagan was **drafted** into the U.S. Army in 1941, but his poor vision kept him from combat. He used his professional talents to make movies for the military instead. The films raised money and helped the war effort by encouraging men to become soldiers.

Family Man

In 1940, Reagan married actress Jane Wyman. The couple had a daughter and adopted a son before divorcing in 1948. He married actress Nancy Davis four years later. They had three more children, one of whom died just nine hours after her birth.

▲ As SAG president, Reagan spoke to the House of Representatives about communism in 1947.

Positioned for Politics

By 1954, Reagan had made dozens of movies. He had served two terms as SAG president. But his film career was slowing down. Reagan wanted a new challenge. This time, he decided to go into politics.

In 1962, Reagan registered as a Republican. His values were **conservative**. He spoke out against the government being too involved in people's lives. He believed in personal freedoms. One of Reagan's political goals was close to his heart. He wanted to stop the spread of communism around the world.

Reagan ran for governor of California in 1966. He won in a clear victory. In his first term, he wanted to balance the budget. To do so, he raised taxes and cut spending.

In 1970, Reagan won a second term as governor. He kept working on the budget. By 1973, the budget had a **surplus**! Reagan was able to give people some money back. Taxpayers in California were thrilled. However, by the time Reagan's second term ended, the country was in a **recession**.

Inherited Illness

Reagan's mother died of Alzheimer's disease in 1962. He was heartbroken to lose her. Alzheimer's disease causes memory loss and mood changes. Scientists believe the disease is passed down through families. Sadly, Reagan would die of the same disease in 2004.

Persistence Pays Off

Reagan knew he wanted to be president. He ran in 1968 and again in 1976. He lost both times. Reagan decided to try again in 1980. He thought his experience balancing California's budget would help him solve the nationwide recession.

▲ Reagan takes the oath of office as governor of California on January 2, 1967.

◀ The Reagans celebrate his election victory.

President Reagan

In 1980, Reagan became the Republican nominee for president. Now, he had to win the election against Democratic **incumbent** President Jimmy Carter. Reagan had strong opinions on what he thought was best for the country. He wanted to fight communism. He thought the economy was in bad shape, and he thought he could fix it.

Many people were drawn to Reagan. People knew him as the hero actor from some of their favorite films. They felt close to Reagan since he had not always been a politician. Voters thought having someone new in the White House could be a good thing.

▼ Reagan and his wife, Nancy, greet the crowd at his first inaugural ball.

In November 1980, voters elected Reagan president of the United States. He set to work trying to fix the economy. Reagan quickly called for budget cuts and tax cuts. He wanted people to have more money to spend. He thought that was the best way to fix the economy. The country was ready for a major change. Reagan was ready to deliver that change.

Iranian Hostage Crisis

In 1979, 66 Americans were taken **hostage** in Iran. They were held for over a year. Many Americans blamed President Carter for this crisis. The hostages were released the day Reagan was sworn in to office.

Temperature Changes

When Reagan was sworn in as president in 1981, he stood in front of the U.S. Capitol building. It was 55 degrees Fahrenheit (13 degrees Celsius) outside. That was the warmest **inauguration** day on record. Large crowds came to see the event. Four years later, Reagan would have a different experience. The temperature on his second inauguration day was 7° F (−14° C). That was the coldest inauguration on record! Reagan had to be sworn in inside due to the freezing weather.

An Attempt on His Life

Hinckley's Reasoning

The **assassination** attempt was committed by a man named John Hinckley Jr (shown below). He was seeking attention from actress Jodie Foster. In her film *Taxi Driver*, the main character tries to shoot a presidential candidate. Hinckley thought shooting Reagan would bring him and Foster together.

Finding Humor

When Nancy Reagan first saw her husband in the hospital, he was pale. Reagan opened his eyes, took off his oxygen mask, and said, "Honey, I forgot to duck." When he was being wheeled into surgery, he had one more joke. Reagan told the doctors that he hoped they were all Republicans.

On March 30, 1981—only two months after being sworn in—Reagan was shot leaving a hotel in Washington, DC. The bullet hit Reagan's lung and barely missed his heart. Reagan had to have surgery to fix the damage.

Within a few weeks of his surgery, Reagan was back at work. He was hailed a hero when he spoke to **Congress** for the first time after the shooting.

▼ Reagan gives a television presentation on his plan to lower taxes in July 1981.

YOUR TAXES
AVERAGE FAMILY INCOME - $20,000

1982

1986

$

THEIR BILL

OUR BILL

His plans for budget cuts, tax cuts, and increased military spending were all well received.

In 1982, the country was in a deep recession. More than nine million Americans were out of work. Reagan believed his policies were still the best way to help the country. He would not cut military spending. However, he did support a tax increase for the first time in his presidency. Reagan also cut government spending on **social programs**. People called his policies "Reaganomics." The U.S. economy began to improve by the next year.

Serving a Second Term

In 1983, Reagan revealed plans for the Strategic Defense Initiative (SDI). The SDI would use high-tech weapons to guard against nuclear attacks. Some weapons would be placed in space. In the end, many of the high-tech ideas were not put into place. Over time, the program was changed to focus on ground-based weapons.

At the same time, Reagan was also running for a second term as president. He ran for re-election against Walter Mondale. Reagan easily won the election. People liked what he had done his first term. One of Reagan's first announcements after he won shocked many people. It was a plan to meet with the leader of the Soviet Union—Konstantin Chernenko (kahn-stan-TEEN chare-NEN-koh).

In the past, Reagan had been clear that he saw the communist Soviet Union as an enemy of the United States. The countries had been at odds since the end of World War II. This period of history was known as the Cold War. The Cold War was not filled with battles and bloodshed. Instead, it was a time of tension between the governments of the Soviet Union and the United States.

▲ Reagan shows his support for the SDI.

Star Wars

From 1977 to 1983, the first three Star Wars movies were released. The films were hugely popular. When Reagan announced his plans to put weapons in space with the SDI, people nicknamed the plan "Star Wars."

Tremendous Triumph

In the 1984 election, Reagan won almost 98 percent of the electoral votes. (*Electoral votes* are votes cast by members of the United States Electoral College). Reagan also won 59 percent of the popular vote. Since then, no other candidate has won that much of the electoral vote or the popular vote.

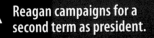

▲ Reagan campaigns for a second term as president.

Iran-Contra Affair

Reagan's sale of weapons to Iran was discovered in 1986. When the situation was investigated, Reagan had to tell his side of the story to Congress. It was clear that he was very confused about the specifics of the plan. Reagan was not charged with a crime.

The Reagan Doctrine

U.S. policy during the Cold War was to stop communism. In the past, presidents had tried to prevent it from spreading. In 1985, Reagan took a stronger stance. He wanted to help people around the world fight communism. He thought this would inspire other nations to fight back. His plan to give military aid was called the Reagan **Doctrine**.

Hostage Crisis in the Air

On June 14, 1985, terrorists hijacked a plane in Athens, Greece. Americans on the plane were held hostage. In public, the United States said it would not negotiate with terrorists. In secret, the trade of weapons for hostages was approved. On June 30, the final 39 passengers were released.

The Reagan Doctrine was successful in Afghanistan. But in Nicaragua, there were problems. Years before the Reagan Doctrine was put into action, Reagan had approved military training of **contras**. Their task was to stop a communist group from gaining power. When members of Congress learned of the contra program, they tried to stop it. However, Reagan kept going. He got money from private donors and foreign governments. He even raised money by selling weapons to Iran. He kept his plans a secret from Congress. Reagan broke the law, but he thought his actions were needed. He felt that it was worth it since he was working toward keeping the country safe.

▼ Anti-communist contras train in Nicaragua in 1985.

Meeting with the Soviets

In the beginning of Reagan's second term, he went to Moscow. He was there to meet with the Soviet leader, Chernenko. They wanted to discuss their future relations. The meeting lasted for less than an hour, but it was still a huge deal. As tensions eased, the two leaders looked for ways to come together.

In March of the next year, the Soviet people elected a new leader. Mikhail Gorbachev (mih-KAYL GOR-buh-chof) was a charming, smart leader. He quickly struck up a bond with Reagan. The two leaders began meeting often. In 1986, Reagan and Gorbachev began speaking about a more peaceful world. It would be a world without nuclear weapons. It would be a world without tension between the two nations. Many Americans were thrilled with the peace talks. However, government leaders were more guarded.

Reagan and Gorbachev kept meeting while Reagan was in office. By the time Reagan's second term ended, the two men had become near **allies**. As Reagan was leaving the presidency, he spoke of the future. He told Americans that Gorbachev was different from past Soviet leaders. Reagan said Gorbachev was trying to fix things, and Reagan wished him well.

Reagan and Gorbachev meet in Iceland in 1986. ▶

▼ People climb on the Berlin Wall as it is taken down in 1989.

The Soviet Union

The Soviet Union was formed in 1922. Its official name was the Union of Soviet Socialist Republics (or the USSR). People have lived in this area for more than four thousand years.

A Famous Quotation

In 1961, the Berlin Wall was built. It encircled West Berlin during the Cold War. West Berlin was under the control of the United States, France, and Great Britain—all democratic governments. East Berlin was under the control of the Soviet Union—a communist government. The wall blocked access between West Berlin and all of East Germany. The Berlin Wall became a famous symbol of communism for decades. In 1987, Reagan gave a speech in Berlin. Thousands of people listened as he spoke his famous words: "Mr. Gorbachev, tear down this wall!" The wall would begin to be taken down just as Reagan was leaving office.

After Reagan

In 1989, Reagan's vice president—George H. W. Bush—was elected president. People worried that the new bonds between the two countries would end. But Gorbachev and Bush continued to meet several times over the next two years. They picked up where Reagan had left off. However, things were about to change in a big way.

Since taking office, Gorbachev had been loosening his government's control over the people. People could speak up without fear for the first time in years. At the time, many people did not have enough food. They blamed the government for not helping them. Other people wanted the government's control to be tightened. They wanted to stay a strong communist country. All these people spoke out against the government.

▼ Bush, Reagan, and Gorbachev meet in 1988 in New York.

Parts of the Soviet Union began to break away and form their own nations. Then, in August 1991, a group gained fame when it tried to remove Gorbachev from office. The plan failed. However, it showed the world that many Soviet people did not like their leader. The Soviet Union continued to break apart with new nations forming every month. In December, Gorbachev stepped down as president. By the end of the year, the Soviet Union had split into 15 different countries. The Soviet Union as the world knew it was gone.

USSR

▲ Soviet Union after World War II

Soviet Union at the end of 1991 ▼

1 RUSSIA
2 ESTONIA
3 LATVIA
4 LITHUANIA
5 BELARUS
6 UKRAINE
7 MOLDOVA
8 GEORGIA
9 ARMENIA
10 AZERBAIJAN
11 KAZAKHSTAN
12 UZBEKISTAN
13 TURKMENISTAN
14 KYRGYZSTAN
15 TAJIKISTAN

Final Years and Legacy

Reagan had spent his last years in office working to build the future he had in mind for the United States and the world. He had encouraged the destruction of the Berlin Wall. He had lessened the number of nuclear weapons in the world. Reagan had also fought for people's freedoms.

▼ Reagan signs the Civil Liberties Act.

In 1988, Reagan was presented with the Civil Liberties Act. The act was an apology. During World War II, Japanese Americans had been treated cruelly. They had been taken from their homes and sent to live in camps. This dark period in American history did not fit with Reagan's more peaceful view of the future. He knew something had to be done. The Civil Liberties Act would give $20,000 and a formal apology to each person sent to the camps during the war. Reagan had spent his time as president trying to save the country money. However, he signed the act into law. At the time, people said Reagan had brought an end to a "civil rights disaster."

There were bumps along the way for Reagan. But he still left office with a 53 percent approval rating. Most Americans felt he had done a good job. It was the highest rating of a president since Lyndon B. Johnson left office in 1969.

Farewell

On January 11, 1989, Reagan gave his final address to the country. He ended with a positive look back at his presidency: "And how stands the city on this winter night? More prosperous, more secure, and happier than it was eight years ago."

Furry Friends

Reagan loved feeding the squirrels that lived just outside the Oval Office. When Bush took office, his family moved into the White House. They brought their dog, Millie, with them. On the Oval Office door, Bush found a note from Reagan to the squirrels that read, "Beware of the dog."

Early Alzheimer's

Reagan's son Ron wrote a book, *My Father at 100*, in 2011. In it, Ron wrote that he believed his dad had Alzheimer's disease while in office. He wrote that he saw signs of confusion and memory loss as early as 1984.

Jelly Beans

Reagan was also nicknamed the "Jelly Bean Man." He began eating jelly beans while governor of California to quit smoking. This candy habit followed him into the White House. Reagan kept a jar of jelly beans near him in meetings in case the need for a snack arose.

After he left office, Reagan's leadership continued to change the country and the world. The Berlin Wall finished coming down. People in the Soviet Union were allowed to elect their leaders. Before, the government chose the president. After Reagan, the power was with the people. Reagan had set out to stop communism. Thanks to his hard work while in office, he made huge strides in making that happen.

After leaving office, Reagan continued to be in the public eye. He gave speeches and pushed for new laws. One speech Reagan gave in 1994 changed everything. Reagan revealed that he had been diagnosed with Alzheimer's disease. The nation was shocked and people mourned. Reagan quickly lost many of his memories, but Americans vowed to never forget the Great Communicator. Reagan had won many hearts both during and after his time in office. He had led the country through a time of great change.

Reagan died on June 5, 2004. A seven-day state funeral was held in his honor. Hundreds of thousands of people came to grieve. Today, Reagan is buried in California. Each year, thousands of people go to his grave to pay their respects to the Gipper.

I KNOW IN MY HEART THAT MAN IS GOOD
THAT WHAT IS RIGHT WILL ALWAYS EVENTUALLY TRIUMPH
AND THERE IS PURPOSE AND WORTH TO EACH AND EVERY LIF

◀ This quotation from Reagan is inscribed
on a monument where he is buried.

Film It!

Reagan's presidency was a time of change for the nation. People have strong feelings about him, both positive and negative. Find someone who lived through Reagan's presidency. Ask relatives, teachers, and neighbors. See if you can find a few people who will let you interview them on camera.

Write a list of questions about what people remember and how they felt about specific events. Consider asking about the presidential debates, the Cold War, meetings with Gorbachev, the fall of the Berlin Wall, and other issues. You might ask how they voted in 1980 and 1984, if they voted at the time.

Let people see your questions before you turn on the camera. That way, they can choose which ones they'd like to answer. Record a few interviews, and combine them into a mini-documentary. Your work will show personal stories about the issues Reagan—and all Americans—faced.

allies—people who join together for a common cause or goal

assassination—an act in which someone is killed

blacklisted—put on a list of people who are not allowed to do something

communism—a political system in which all property is owned by the government

Congress—the group of people who work in the U.S. Senate and the U.S. House of Representatives and who make the nation's laws

conservative—having political and societal beliefs that are seen as traditional

contras—members of groups who oppose governments

degree—an official document or title given to someone who has completed classes at a university or college

dispute—a disagreement

doctrine—a government policy, usually in regards to international relations

drafted—selected for military service from the general population

hostage—captured by someone who demands things to be done before th person is freed

inauguration—an act or ceremony tha is part of introducing someone into a particular position or office

incumbent—a person who currently holds a particular position or office

recession—a period of time in which there is a decrease in economic activity and many people do not have jobs

scholarship—money that is given to a student to help pay for the student's education

social programs—government-funded programs that help people find housing, food, and other necessary things

sociology—the study of societies

Sunday school—religious classes held on Sundays

surplus—an amount more than the amount needed

wit—ability to write or say things that are clever and usually funny

Index

THERE IS ONE SIGN THE SOVIETS CAN MAKE THAT WOULD BE UNMISTAKABLE, THAT WOULD ADVANCE DRAMATICALLY THE CAUSE OF FREEDOM AND PEACE.

GENERAL SECRETARY GORBACHEV, IF YOU SEEK PEACE — IF YOU SEEK PROSPERITY FOR THE SOVIET UNION AND EASTERN EUROPE — IF YOU SEEK LIBERALIZATION: COME HERE, TO THIS GATE.

MR. GORBACHEV, OPEN THIS GATE.

MR. GORBACHEV, TEAR DOWN THIS WALL.

I UNDERSTAND THE FEAR OF WAR AND THE PAIN OF DIVISION THAT AFFLICT THIS CONTINENT — AND I PLEDGE TO YOU MY COUNTRY'S EFFORTS TO HELP OVERCOME THESE BURDENS. TO BE SURE, WE IN THE WEST MUST RESIST SOVIET EXPANSION. SO WE MUST MAINTAIN DEFENSES OF UNASSAILABLE STRENGTH. YET WE SEEK PEACE. SO WE MUST STRIVE TO REDUCE ARMS ON BOTH SIDES.

Your Turn!

Ronald Reagan was known for his quick wit and funny jokes. However, when he spoke to a crowd of more than ten thousand people in front of the Berlin Wall, his tone was more serious. Imagine you are in front of that crowd. What do you want to say to the people of Berlin? What do you want to say to your new ally, Gorbachev? Write a speech as if you were Reagan. Then, deliver your speech to a friend or family member. Remember to act like the Great Communicator during your delivery.